CAMARASAURUS

A Buddy Book
by
Michael P. Goecke

ABDO
Publishing Company

VISIT US AT

www.abdopublishing.com

Published by ABDO Publishing Company, 4940 Viking Drive, Edina, Minnesota 55435.

Copyright © 2007 by Abdo Consulting Group, Inc. International copyrights reserved in all countries. No part of this book may be reproduced in any form without written permission from the publisher. Buddy Books™ is a trademark and logo of ABDO Publishing Company.

Printed in the United States.

Edited by: Sarah Tieck
Graphic Design: Denise Esner
Cover Art: Deb Coldiron, title page
Interior Photos/Illustrations: Pages 5 & 12: Natural History Museum; pages 6 & 18: Maria Hosley; pages 8 & 9: Mineo Shiraishi; Page 11: Carnegie Museum of Natural History; pages 15, 19, 20 & 21: Photos.com; page 17: ©Julius T. Csotonyi; pages 23 & 25: Joe Tucciarone; page 27: Stringer/Getty Images.

Library of Congress Cataloging-in-Publication Data

Goecke, Michael P., 1968-
    Camarasaurus / Michael P. Goecke
      p. cm. — (Dinosaurs)
    Includes index.
    ISBN-13: 978-1-59928-695-2
    ISBN-10: 1-59928-695-5
     1. Camarasaurus—Juvenile literature. I. Title.

QE862.S3G633 2007
567.913—dc22

                                                                    2006032068

TABLE OF CONTENTS

WHAT WAS IT?

Millions of years ago, Earth was a very different place. There were no cars or buildings. And, dinosaurs walked the land.

One of those dinosaurs was the Camarasaurus. It lived in North America about 150 million years ago. This was during the Late **Jurassic period**.

Camarasaurus
KAM-ah-rah-SAWR-uhs

5

The Camarasaurus was a long-necked, long-tailed dinosaur. It had a small head with a short, rounded **snout**. Two large nostrils sat on top of its snout, in front of its eyes. Its teeth were spoon shaped.

The Camarasaurus's head was small compared to its body.

The Camarasaurus was about 65 feet (20 m) long. That is about the same length as a sperm whale.

The Camarasaurus was around 65 feet (20 m) long. It weighed as much as 40,000 pounds (18,000 kg).

The Camarasaurus was very large. Scientists say it probably walked quite slowly on its four thick legs.

TAIL

Its front legs were a little shorter than its back legs. Even so, the Camarasaurus walked with its back almost level to the ground.

The Camarasaurus had five toes on each foot. Both front feet had a long, sharp claw.

HEAD

This claw was located on its inner toe. Scientists think the Camarasaurus used these claws for protection.

LEG

FOOT

9

WHY WAS IT SPECIAL?

The Camarasaurus was a sauropod. Sauropods were a group of dinosaurs with long necks and long tails. They were also **herbivores**.

Sauropods were very large dinosaurs. But, the Camarasaurus was small compared to most sauropods.

The Camarasaurus was also lighter for its size. This is because some of its bones were hollow. These bones were in its back. The bones in the back are called **vertebrae**.

Human vertebrae.

The Camarasaurus had hollow vertebrae in its neck. This allowed it to lift its head more easily.

The Camarasaurus had an unusual **skull**. It was arched. This means that it was high and rounded. Most sauropods had flat heads. So, the Camarasaurus was **unique**.

Unlike many other sauropods, the Camarasaurus had an arched head.

The Camarasaurus's **skull** had many holes, like a sponge. But scientists do not think it was weak.

The name Camarasaurus means "chambered lizard." This name describes the Camarasaurus's bones. It comes from the hollow **vertebrae** and the arched skull with holes.

LAND OF THE CAMARASAURUS

The Camarasaurus lived in North America. North America was very different during the Late **Jurassic period**.

There were a lot of plants where the Camarasaurus lived. This was important because there were many herbivorous dinosaurs.

Some of the plants in the land of the Camarasaurus were conifers, or evergreens. Ginkgoes and cycads were there, too. There were also many ferns. Some tree ferns grew very tall. Others were small and just covered the ground.

Evergreens

Ginkgo

Many other sauropods lived with the Camarasaurus. These were enormous dinosaurs such as the Apatosaurus, the Brachiosaurus, and the Diplodocus.

The Apatosaurus grew up to 90 feet (27 m) long. And, it weighed up to 70,000 pounds (32,000 kg). The Brachiosaurus was even heavier! It weighed 130,000 pounds (59,000 kg) and was almost 50 feet (15 m) tall. That is as high as a five-story building!

The Diplodocus was about 90 feet (27 m) long. It looked a lot like the Apatosaurus. But, its tail was half its entire length! In fact, some scientists believe the Diplodocus used its tail as a whip to protect itself.

The Diplodocus was a larger sauropod neighbor of the Camarasaurus.

WHAT DID IT EAT?

The Camarasaurus was an **herbivore**. A wide variety of plants lived during its time. But, scientists say that the Camarasaurus ate only certain plants. They think the Camarasaurus probably ate rough plants. Other sauropods and herbivorous dinosaurs ate softer plants.

Camarasaurus teeth.

Chisel

The Camarasaurus had strong, chisel-like teeth. Scientists have studied these teeth and the teeth of other sauropods. They have found tiny, **unique** scratches on sauropod teeth. These scratches help scientists understand what kind of food each sauropod might have eaten.

Scientists think that the Camarasaurus swallowed plants whole. Also, it may have swallowed rough stones called gastroliths.

These helped break up the food inside its stomach.

The Camarasaurus may have eaten stones like these to break down food inside its stomach.

Today, birds such as the grouse eat stones to break down their food.

After the gastroliths became smooth, the Camarasaurus may have **expelled** them from its body. Piles of unusually smooth stones have been found near Camarasaurus **fossils**.

The Camarasaurus lived among many dinosaurs. Not all of them were plant-eaters. Some hunted and ate meat.

The Allosaurus was a large meat-eating dinosaur. It preyed on other dinosaurs, including the Camarasaurus. In fact, the Allosaurus was the biggest **carnivore** of its time.

The Allosaurus was about 38 feet (12 m) long. It weighed about 4,000 pounds (1,800 kg). This is much smaller than the Camarasaurus.

So, how could the Allosaurus have hunted the Camarasaurus? The Allosaurus was fast. It could probably run about 20 miles (32 km) per hour. And, it had many sharp teeth. Scientists also think that the Allosaurus might have hunted in groups.

Allosaurus

THE CAMARASAURUS FAMILY

The Camarasaurus is part of the sauropod family. Sauropods were the largest dinosaurs. They walked on four thick legs. And, they were **herbivores**.

Camarasaurus is one of the smallest sauropods. Apatosaurus and Diplodocus were larger than Camarasaurus. The Seismosaurus and the Supersaurus were even bigger.

Scientists believe the Argentinosaurus was one of the biggest land animals ever. It weighed more than 180,000 pounds (82,000 kg)! This giant sauropod lived in South America.

Argentinosaurus

RAISING ITS YOUNG

Fossil evidence shows that the Camarasaurus did not lay eggs in a nest. Instead, it laid them in a row as it walked along. And, scientists believe the Camarasaurus, like many sauropods, did not care for its young.

Scientists say that when young dinosaurs grew older and larger, they joined the adults. Fossil discoveries show both large and small Camarasaurus dinosaurs together. This tells scientists that both adult and younger dinosaurs lived together in herds.

DISCOVERY

In 1877, Oramel W. Lucas found the first Camarasaurus **fossils** in Colorado. Following his discovery, Lucas wrote a letter to **paleontologist** Edward Drinker Cope. Cope studied the dinosaur and named it Camarasaurus.

Since that time, Camarasaurus fossils have been discovered in New Mexico, Utah, and Wyoming.

Edward Drinker Cope

Carnegie Museum of Natural History
4400 Forbes Ave.
Pittsburgh, PA 15213
http://www.carnegiemnh.org

Peabody Museum of Natural History
Yale University
New Haven, CT 06520
http://www.yale.edu/peabody/

CAMARASAURUS

NAME MEANS	Chambered lizard
DIET	Plants
WEIGHT	40,000 pounds (18,000 kg)
LENGTH	65 feet (20 m)
TIME	Late Jurassic period
OTHER SAUROPODS	Diplodocus, Apatosaurus
SPECIAL FEATURE	Hollow vertebrae
FOSSILS FOUND	Colorado, New Mexico, Utah, and Wyoming

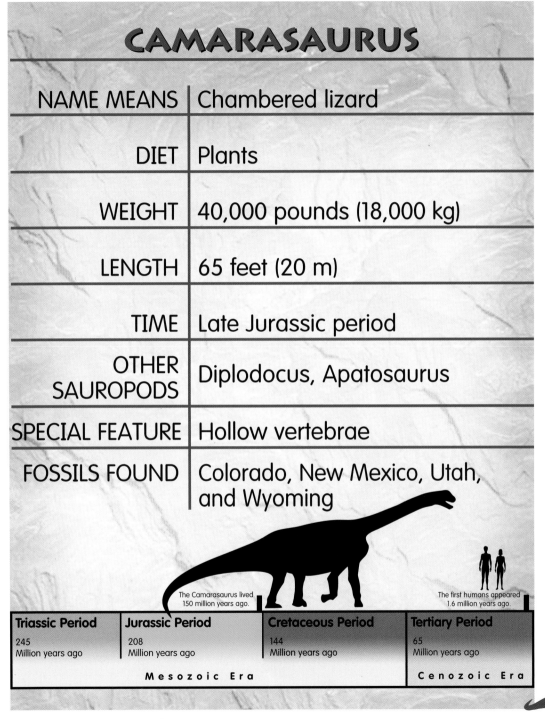

The Camarasaurus lived 150 million years ago.

The first humans appeared 1.6 million years ago.

Triassic Period	Jurassic Period	Cretaceous Period	Tertiary Period
245 Million years ago	208 Million years ago	144 Million years ago	65 Million years ago
Mesozoic Era			Cenozoic Era

WEB SITES

To learn more about the Camarasaurus, visit ABDO Publishing Company on the World Wide Web. Web sites about the Camarasaurus are featured on our "Book Links" page. These links are routinely monitored and updated to provide the most current information available.

www.abdopublishing.com

carnivore a meat-eater.

evidence facts that prove something is true.

expel to push out of the body.

fossil remains of very old animals and plants commonly found in the ground. A fossil can be a bone, a footprint, or any trace of life.

herbivore a plant-eater.

Jurassic period a period of time that happened 208–144 million years ago.

paleontologist someone who studies very old life, such as dinosaurs, mostly by studying fossils.

skull the bony part of the head that protects the brain.

snout the part of the face that sticks out including the nose and the jaws.

unique the only one of its kind.

vertebra one of the bones that make up the spine.

INDEX